**Observe and Prompt**

**Word Recognition**

- Ask the children what Kim is doing at this point in the story.
- How do the children think Kim is feeling? How can they tell?
- What do they think Kim might want the rug for?

What does she get now?

Where is she making her den?

## 👁 Observe and Prompt

### Word Recognition

- Check the children can read the words 'She' and 'a'. (These are sight words – words likely to be in their store of familiar words.)

- The word 'pillow' may not be fully decodable for the children at this stage. If they struggle, ask them if they recognise the initial letter and sound – 'p'. Then tell them this word and model the reading of it for them.

**Observe and Prompt**

**Language Comprehension**

- Ask the children what Kim is getting now.
- What do the children think Kim is making?

## Observe and Prompt

### Word Recognition

- The word 'chair' may not be decodable for the children at the stage. Ask them if they recognise the initial letters and sound - 'ch'. Then tell them the word and model the reading of it for them.

## Observe and Prompt

### Language Comprehension

- Observe that the children have noticed the text pattern.
- Ask the children what Kim is getting now.

What does she get now?

 **Observe and Prompt**

## Word Recognition

- If children struggle with the word 'stool', prompt them to identify the initial letter and sound – 's'. Then prompt them to read the adjacent consonants 'st' and continue blending the sounds all through the word.

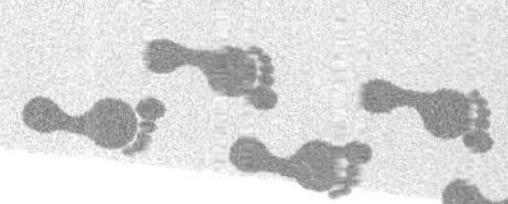

## Observe and Prompt

**Language Comprehension**

- Check the children understand what is happening in the story now.

- Ask the children what Kim has got so far.

- What do the children think she might get next?

**Walkthrough**

What does she get now?

What else does she get?

Does she need anything else to make it into
a proper den?

She gets a box.

10

 **Observe and Prompt**

**Word Recognition**

- Check the children are using their decoding skills to read
  the CVC word 'box'. Can they sound out and blend b-o-x all
  through the word?

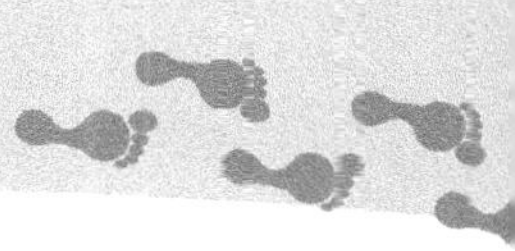

11



## Observe and Prompt

**Language Comprehension**

- Ask the children what Kim has got now.

- Do the children think Kim's den is almost ready?

- What else do the children think Kim might need to get?

**Walkthrough**

What does she get now?

What could she use the umbrella for?

She gets an umbrella.

12

 **Observe and Prompt**

### Word Recognition

- Check whether the children say 'a' or 'an'. If they say 'a' ask them to look at the word again, pointing out the 'n'.

- Prompt the children to use their decoding skills to read the word 'umbrella'. Ask them to blend the sounds from left to right, through the word. Assist the children if they struggle with the double 'll'.

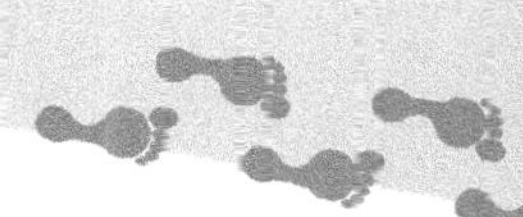

## Observe and Prompt

### Language Comprehension

- Ask the children what they think Kim will use the umbrella for.
- Do the children think it looks like a den yet?

She gets a big sheet.

14

 **Observe and Prompt**

**Word Recognition**

- Check the children are reading 'big' using their decoding skills.
  Can they sound out and blend b-i-g all through the word?

- If the children struggle with the word 'sheet', ask them if
  they recognise the initial letters and sound – 'sh'. Then
  prompt them to use their decoding skills to read the word,
  blending the sounds from left to right through the word.

15

## Observe and Prompt

**Language Comprehension**

- Do the children think the den is finished now?
- Ask the children if they have ever made a den ike this.
- What do the children think Kim will do now?

**Walkthrough**

Now what does Kim do?

What do you think of Kim's den?

Is it like any of your dens?

 **Observe and Prompt**

### Word Recognition

- Check the children can read the sight words 'in' and 'her'.

- Check the children are reading 'den' using their decoding skills. Can they sound out and blend d-e-n all through the word?

### Language Comprehension

- Ask the children what happened at the end of the story.

- How do the children think Kim is feeling?

- Do the children like Kim's den?